Amelia Earhart

Amelia Earhart
Aviation Pioneer

Roxane Chadwick

Lerner Publications Company ■ Minneapolis

This book is available in two editions:
Library binding by Lerner Publications Company
Soft cover by First Avenue Editions
241 First Avenue North
Minneapolis, Minnesota 55401

To Amy

LIBRARY OF CONGRESS CATALOGING-IN-PUBLICATION DATA

Chadwick, Roxane.
　Amelia Earhart : aviation pioneer.

　(The Achievers)
　Summary: Traces the life of the pilot who became the first
woman to fly across the Atlantic Ocean.
　1. Earhart, Amelia, 1897-1937—Juvenile literature. 2. Air
pilots—United States—Biography—Juvenile literature. [1.
Earhart, Amelia, 1897-1937. 2. Air pilots] I. Title. II. Series.
TL540.E3C47 1987　　629.13′092′4 [B] [92]　　87-4241
ISBN 0-8225-0484-7 (lib. bdg.)
ISBN 0-8225-9515-X (pbk.)

Manufactured in the United States of America

International Standard Book Number: 0-8225-0484-7 (lib. bdg.)
International Standard Book Number: 0-8225-9515-X (pbk.)
Library of Congress Catalog Card Number: 87-4241

4　5　6　7　8　9　97　96　95　94　93　92

Amelia in 1903 at age five

Early one morning, Edwin Earhart and his daughter Amelia Mary walked down a dirt street in Atchison, Kansas. Dressed in dark blue, knee-length bloomers, Amelia carried a bamboo pole, from which dangled three, freshly-caught fish.

Any "proper" ladies of Atchison watching the seven-year-old might have been shocked. After all, in 1905, little girls were expected to wear long skirts with ribbons and laces, to play quietly with dolls, and to learn how to cook and sew. They certainly did *not* wear bloomers and go fishing.

Amelia (right) and Muriel in their "shocking" bloomers

Mr. Earhart, however, allowed Amelia and her younger sister, Muriel, to do many things usually reserved for boys. He let them play baseball, explore caves, fish, walk on stilts, and collect insects, worms, and toads.

Amelia's mother, Amy Earhart, liked adventures, too. She had been the first woman to climb to the top of Pike's Peak in Colorado. She was the daughter of Alfred Otis, an influential Kansas judge who had helped to establish the town of Atchison. Judge Otis had expected his daughter to be a belle of Atchison society, so he was disappointed when she married Edwin Earhart, the son of a minister.

Amelia was born in her grandpa Otis's large white house on Quality Hill, where many prominent and wealthy

Amelia's birthplace and childhood home

people lived. She spent much of her childhood there because her father, a lawyer for the railroads, was frequently away on business, and her mother often traveled with him. The house sat on a bluff overlooking the Missouri River, surrounded by gardens. It was a perfect place for curious little girls.

Although her sense of adventure and her daring often got her into trouble, young Amelia never let that stop her from doing what she wanted. "I am sure I was a horrid little girl," she wrote years later.

When she was nine, Amelia asked her father for a boy's sled for Christmas. Not for Amelia were the lightweight, boxy sleds that girls rode only on gentle slopes. Instead, she got the sled she had requested. She then sped down steep hills, steering around trees as well as any boy.

For adventure one spring, Amelia decided to build a roller coaster. She coaxed her sister and a few friends into helping her build a rickety ramp from an eight-foot-high woodshed to the ground. Then Amelia, the test pilot, got in the "car"—a square board with two parallel planks on the underside—and headed for her first crash landing. Undaunted, she made adjustments and kept trying until she completed a successful ride. "It's just like flying!" she said.

Other inventors of the early 1900s had better luck with their flying inventions, however. In 1903, Orville Wright had flown the first gasoline-powered airplane for 12 seconds and a distance of 120 feet (36 meters). Two years later,

The first powered flight was made by the Wright brothers on December 17, 1903.

the Wright brothers had built a plane that could turn in circles and do figure-eights in the sky. One of their longer flights lasted 38 minutes and covered 24 miles (38 kilometers). By 1908, airplanes could climb and turn, but they were still difficult to control.

Ten-year-old Amelia saw a flying machine for the first time in 1908 at the Iowa State Fair. The biplane had double wings and was built of wood, wire, and oiled canvas. It basically resembled a large box kite. The pilot of this early airplane sat near the front of the contraption, resting his feet on the nearest brace. Goggles masked his face to protect his eyes from the wind, and the engine sputtered behind him. Amelia was not very impressed when the plane bumped along the ground, then floundered into the air. She may have been thinking that she could build something better.

Although Amelia was the tow-headed tomboy of Quality Hill, she loved to spend time reading. In fact, she finished most of the books in her grandfather's large library. The many hours she spent reading instead of getting into trouble provided some much-needed quiet time for the entire household.

Amelia's carefree exploration of the open land on Quality Hill ended when the Earharts moved to Des Moines,

Amelia (left) and Muriel Earhart with their father and the family cook on Earhart's private railroad car, 1910

Iowa, in 1909. There Mr. Earhart became head of the Rock Island Railroad's claims department and was provided with a private railway car. In it, the Earhart family took trips to Kansas City, St. Paul, Chicago, and even California. Amelia loved traveling, seeing new places and meeting new people.

During the Earharts' three years in Des Moines, however, Edwin Earhart developed a serious problem with alcohol. His drinking strained his family life and ruined his promising career. Because he could no longer find work as a lawyer, Mr. Earhart accepted a job as a clerk for the Great Northern Railway in St. Paul, Minnesota. His family moved with him and hoped the situation would improve, but he soon lost that job, too. When Earhart was promised a better position in the claims department of the Burlington Road in Springfield, Missouri, the family packed up once again. But when they reached Springfield, they found the job was not available after all. At that point, Mrs. Earhart and her daughters went to Chicago to stay with friends, while Mr. Earhart moved to Kansas City to live with his sister and try to start a law office.

These were terrible and uncertain years for Amelia, now in her early teens. But instead of becoming bitter— as she easily might have—she developed compassion for people with drinking problems.

Amelia finished high school in Chicago in 1916. Although she had attended six different high schools during her family's moves, she worked hard to graduate on schedule.

The caption in her Hyde Park High yearbook called her "the girl in brown who walks alone." Although the caption was not very flattering, it was accurate. Amelia often wore practical brown clothes, and she had been a loner.

After high school, Amelia hoped to go to the Ogontz School in Rydal, Pennsylvania, but her family lacked the necessary funds. Instead, the Earhart women moved to Kansas City to join Edwin Earhart, who had overcome his drinking problem and started a successful law practice. Soon after they arrived, Mrs. Earhart was granted some inheritance money and was then able to send Amelia to the Ogontz School.

Amelia's stay at the fashionable school was short, however. During Christmas vacation in 1917, she visited her sister, Muriel, who was attending St. Margaret's College in Toronto, Canada. While out for a walk one day, Amelia encountered four men on crutches. They were Canadians who had been wounded fighting overseas. Although World War I had been raging in Europe for three years, meeting the injured men made it seem much closer. Amelia felt she had to help, so she quit school and became a nurse's aide at the Spadina Military Hospital in Toronto.

At the hospital, some of Amelia's patients were military pilots who had taken part in aerial dogfights over the battlefields of Europe. Their stories of daring air-to-air combat sparked Amelia's curiosity about airplanes.

While off duty one afternoon, Amelia joined the crowds at the Toronto Fair to watch ace pilots perform stunts

During World War I, Amelia was a nurses' aid in Toronto.

in their brightly colored planes. The biplanes circled in the air, spun toward the ground, and then looped back up into the clouds. Sometimes the planes swooped close to the spectators, causing people to scatter in all directions. While watching one plane dive toward her, Amelia marveled at the aircraft and what a thrill flying must be. Soon afterward, the 18-year-old signed up for a course in automobile engine mechanics because she wanted to learn just how engines worked.

Amelia had seen airplanes used for war and for stunt flying. Now she saw airplanes used for "joy-hopping." Pilots would take a few brave passengers for short rides and taught hardier students how to fly. As yet, however, no one had thought of using airplanes for transportation.

After the armistice ended World War I in 1919, Amelia studied medicine at Columbia University in New York. Although she did well, she could not forget airplanes. At the end of her first school year, she moved to Los Angeles where her parents were living, intending to finish her medical training there. After visiting an air show with her father, however, she changed her mind and signed up for flying lessons.

Before long, Amelia took her first airplane ride with Frank Hawks, a famous record-setting pilot. After that, she knew she had to fly.

Flying lessons were expensive in 1920. To pay for them, Earhart worked for the telephone company as a file clerk. Her flight instructor was Neta Snook, the first woman to

Earhart after her first solo flight

graduate from the Curtiss School of Aviation. She was a good teacher, and Earhart was a quick student. In the summer of 1922, Amelia got her pilot's license, which made her one of about a dozen licensed women fliers in the world.

In the early days of aviation, pilots spent more time working on their oily engines than in the air. So when she flew, Earhart would don the flying clothes worn by men—boots, goggles, and a leather jacket—because they were practical for flying and fixing planes. Amelia wasn't bothered by some people's disapproval of her unladylike attire. After all, the young woman who had worn bloomers as a little girl was used to dressing to suit her adventures.

Because Earhart did not have enough money to rent an airplane as often as she wanted, she took a job driving a truck for a sand-and-gravel company to pay for more flying time. On July 24, 1922, her 24th birthday, Amelia's mother and sister came to her rescue and helped her buy a bright yellow biplane called a Kinner Canary. Now she could fly whenever she wanted.

Amelia practiced flying until she could easily control her plane, no matter what position it was in. First, she did stalls—a nose-up position that causes a plane's wings to stop producing lift, or upward force. As the plane loses lift, the pilot lowers the nose, gains speed, and tries not to lose too much altitude. Next, she practiced a spin—a dive toward the ground while the plane revolves around the line of descent.

Then Earhart learned how to land with the engine turned off. Once she had mastered the engine-off landing, she knew that any time her engine failed, she could make a safe landing. Finally, to prepare herself for any weather condition she might meet, she flew through fog, rain, sunshine, and snow.

One Sunday in October of 1922, Amelia mysteriously handed her father and sister tickets to an air show.

When they were seated in the bleachers, they heard an announcement that Miss Amelia Earhart was going to try to set a new woman's altitude record. A sealed barograph—an instrument for measuring altitude—was placed in the Canary. Then Amelia soared to 14,000 feet (4,200 m), or almost 3 miles, setting a new record before her engine quit. Amelia did not panic but calmly turned off the fuel switches so there would be no fuel to catch on fire if the landing caused sparks. All of her practice landings without power paid off, and she safely returned to the airfield. Her record, however, stood for only a few weeks.

In spite of her flying skills, Earhart could not find a paying job in aviation. There was little employment for male pilots, and even less for females. Although she worked at a variety of jobs to pay for her flying, Amelia was not able to earn enough to meet the high cost of owning a plane, so she eventually had to sell the Canary and give up flying for a while. Then when her parents divorced, Amelia bought a car and drove her mother and sister across the United States to Boston.

For the next several years, Earhart drifted back and forth between school and jobs, watching from the sidelines while aviators tested their planes on long-distance flights. The most exciting flight happened on May 21, 1927, when Charles Lindbergh became the first person to fly alone across the Atlantic Ocean. Lindbergh had flown from New York to Paris—a distance of 3,610 miles (5,776 km)—in 33 hours and 30 minutes.

Charles Lindbergh on May 20, 1927, ready to take off on his historic flight from New York to Paris in the *Spirit of St. Louis*

Just after Lindbergh's flight, Mrs. Frederick Guest, a flying enthusiast from London, England, decided a woman should cross the Atlantic, too. Hoping to make the historic flight herself, she bought a big plane and named it the *Friendship* to symbolize the goodwill that existed between the United States and Great Britain. When Mrs. Guest's children asked her not to undertake the risky flight, she hired Captain Hilton Railey and George Palmer Putman, a book publisher, to find a woman whose appearance and personality would please the financial backers in London.

At that time, Amelia was employed as a social worker in Boston. There she taught English and played games with immigrant children at a settlement house. One day, she received a phone call from Captain Railey, who asked her if she would be interested in flying across the Atlantic Ocean. Earhart agreed to meet him, and Railey was immediately impressed with her intelligence, her poise, and especially her resemblance to Charles Lindbergh. Amelia had the same light-colored, tousled hair, shyness, and all-American grin as Lindbergh. Next, Earhart was sent to New York for an interview with a three-man panel. Two days later, she received a letter saying she had been selected to cross the Atlantic in the *Friendship*.

Although Amelia was a good pilot, she would not be flying the *Friendship* during any part of the flight. Instead, she would be strictly a passenger. The pilot, Wilmer Stultz, and the mechanic, Lou Gordon, were being paid. Earhart's only reward was the adventure and the fame the flight would bring her. Although three women had already died trying to cross the Atlantic, Earhart looked forward to the dangerous undertaking. If the flight were successful, she would become the first woman to fly as a passenger across the Atlantic Ocean.

The body of the *Friendship* was painted red-orange, and its wings were gold. The bright colors were deliberately chosen so rescue crews could spot the plane if it went down in the ocean. The plane, a Fokker Trimotor, also had pontoons that enabled it to float. Despite these safety precautions, the flight was very dangerous. Radio equipment was primitive, and weather information was unreliable. Deicers had not yet been developed, so the ice crystals that formed on the plane's wings when flying in the cooler air high above the earth's surface were a threat, as icing could cause a plane to lose its ability to fly.

Plans for the expedition were kept secret. While the *Friendship* was readied for the trip, the crew waited in Boston. On June 3, 1928, the *Friendship* and crew flew to Trepassey Bay, Newfoundland, the starting point for the long flight. Then, for 12 days, the crew had to wait there because bad weather prevented their take off. The tension grew unbearable, and Wilmer Stultz drank heavily, reminding Amelia of her father's problems with alcohol.

Finally, on June 17, 1928, the weather cleared. Stultz was in bad condition from his drinking the night before, but Amelia chose not to withdraw from the flight. On the fourth try, the heavily loaded plane got off the ground, and, four hours later, fog hid the choppy ocean below. The aviators checked their position by radio and found they were on course. At 8:00 P.M., however, their radio went dead. During the cloudy night, Stultz flew by the plane's instruments: a compass, an airspeed indicator, and an altimeter, which measured altitude.

When dawn came, the three pilots could only guess at their location. They knew they were over the Atlantic Ocean, and they hoped they were heading toward England. Earhart sighted a luxury liner, but the ship was cutting across the *Friendship's* path instead of sailing parallel to it. If the *Friendship* were on course, a ship crossing the ocean would be going in the same direction. As the *Friendship* circled above the liner, Wilmer Stultz tried fruitlessly to make radio contact. They circled again, hoping the ship's crew might paint their position on the deck, as ships often did for pilots.

When the *Friendship* was too low on fuel to circle much more, Amelia, in desperation, wrapped an orange in a note requesting the boat's position. She put the orange in a paper bag and threw it toward the ship. Unfortunately, her missile fell short of its mark and splashed into the water.

Because the ocean was too choppy for the *Friendship* to land, even with pontoons, the plane headed in the direction that Stultz hoped would lead to shore. With only an hour's worth of fuel left, Stultz finally shouted, "Land!" and set the plane down in a harbor off the coast of Burry

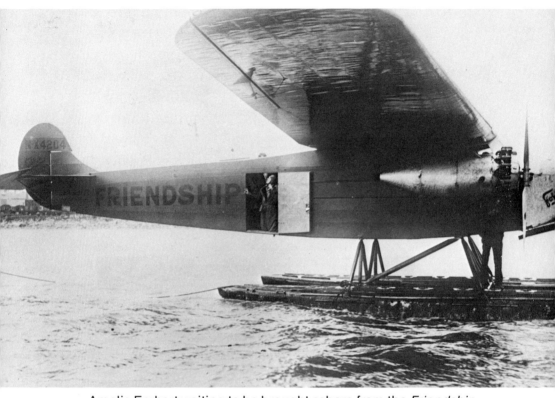

Amelia Earhart waiting to be brought ashore from the *Friendship*

Point, Wales. The *Friendship* had made the crossing in 20 hours and 40 minutes, and Amelia Earhart had become the first woman to cross the Atlantic Ocean by air.

The "welcome" for the three weary aviators was surprising. Wilmer Stultz tied the *Friendship* to a buoy about one-half mile offshore, but no one took any notice of the big red-and-gold seaplane. The crew waited and waited, but no boats came out to greet them.

After a while, Earhart said, "I'll get a boat." She squeezed forward in the cockpit and waved a white towel, her signal of distress, out of the open window. A friendly man on shore took off his coat and waved it back at Amelia—and then returned to his work. The aviators wondered if they would have to swim to shore. Finally, a boat came out to get the *Friendship*'s crew.

Now Amelia Earhart was suddenly famous. Her name and photograph were in newspapers all over the world. She smiled modestly at the adoring crowds but gave full credit for the flight's success to Stultz and Gordon. The reporters nicknamed her "Lady Lindy" because she resembled Charles Lindbergh—a similarity encouraged by the flight's promoters, Railey and Putnam.

When Earhart, Stultz, and Gordon returned to New York City, they were given a hero's welcome. They rode down Broadway in an open car in a ticker-tape parade.

Fame brought Amelia offers to give lectures and demonstrations, to write articles, and to advertise products. But she had already promised to write a book about the flight for her friend, publisher-promoter George Putnam. The volume was called *20 Hours, 40 Minutes: Our Flight in the Friendship*. After Earhart had finished the book, Putnam became her manager. His shrewd business sense made Amelia financially comfortable, and she was able to buy a small plane.

One of Earhart's ambitions was to encourage women to participate in aviation. With her friend Ruth Nicols, she formed a women's flying organization, the Ninety-Nines, named for the 99 charter members. In 1929, Amelia was elected the group's first president.

Earhart also wanted to promote the developing passenger airline industry, so she joined Transcontinental Air Transport (TAT) as an advisor responsible for persuading women that flying was safe. When TAT inaugurated its coast-to-coast passenger service, Amelia met her hero, Charles Lindbergh, and his wife, Anne Morrow Lindbergh. Colonel Lindbergh piloted the company's first flight going west from Winslow, Arizona, to Los Angeles, California, and Amelia and Anne were passengers. Amelia admired Anne, who was a fellow pilot and writer, and who, in Amelia's opinion, had an ideal marriage.

Soon afterwards, George Putnam asked Earhart to marry him. But A.E.—as Putnam called her—was wary because of the unhappiness of her parents' marriage. With the exception of the Lindberghs, Amelia had seen few happy marriages, and she also felt a conventional marriage would interfere with her career. She refused Putnam—or G.P.— several times, but he continued to propose.

When Amelia finally realized Putnam was willing to give her the freedom she needed, she accepted his marriage proposal. Theirs was not to be a conventional marriage, however. Just before the ceremony, the bride, wearing an old brown suit, asked G.P. to sign an unusual agreement. It stated that if they found no happiness together within a year, he would release her from the marriage.

Amelia Earhart (left) with Anne Morrow Lindbergh in California, 1930

A.E. and G.P.

G.P. agreed to Earhart's terms, and they were married in Noank, Connecticut, on February 4, 1931.

Amelia and George became a formidable team, determined to get Earhart what she needed to further her flying career. In one of the many advertising campaigns that G.P. arranged, Earhart flew an autogiro, an aircraft that was part airplane and part helicopter. In this odd-looking machine, A.E. climbed to a record 18,451 feet (5,535 m), or about 3½ miles. Then she flew the autogiro across the United States.

Earhart was the first woman to fly an autogiro.

On June 6, 1931, in Oakland, California, an enthusiastic crowd greeted Earhart on the completion of the first transcontinental auto-giro flight by a woman.

With G.P.'s continued good business guidance and her own growing fame, Earhart no longer needed to worry about money for planes and equipment. She was soon able to buy her dream plane—a high-winged Lockheed Vega, which was perfect for long-distance flying. The single-engine plane was painted red with gold stripes down the body and wings. With its extra wingtanks, it could fly 3,200 miles (5,120 km) without refueling.

Earhart, however, had always felt there was something fraudulent about her fame. Although she was considered the premier woman flier of the world, she had done nothing except ride in the *Friendship.* For four years after that flight, she trained so she could prove she really was the first woman in aviation. Amelia Earhart was getting ready to fly over the Atlantic—but this time alone and without pontoons.

Five years to the day after Lindbergh started his historic flight, Earhart began her solo transatlantic flight. At dusk on May 20, 1932, she took off in her Vega from Harbor Grace, Newfoundland, heading east. Trouble began about 11:00 P.M. when her altimeter failed. Without it, Amelia could not tell how far her plane was above the ocean. To make matters worse, flames began shooting from a broken weld in the engine exhaust.

Used to the hazards of long flights, Earhart now weighed the capabilities of her plane and her own highly developed skills against the troubles of the flight. She chose to go on. One-half hour later, the Vega plunged into a storm. Rough air bounced the plane around, and Amelia could see nothing through the windshield. The storm raged during the long night. At dawn, Earhart tried to take the aircraft above the storm, but ice formed on the wings. To melt the ice. A.E. spun the Vega down toward warmer air. When she finally broke through the clouds, she was about to hit the sea but managed to pull the plane into level flight just above the waves.

Throughout the flight, the fire in the exhaust continued. The plane vibrated heavily, but it held together. Finally, Earhart saw land. She circled and touched down in a cow pasture. Three people from a nearby farmhouse greeted her and told her she was in Ireland. Amelia Earhart had become the first woman to fly solo across the Atlantic and the first woman to cross the ocean twice by air. "It may not all be plain sailing," she said, "but the fun of it is worth the price."

The independent girl from Kansas had now become a self-assured aviator known all over the world. While she

Amelia Earhart's Lockheed Vega is displayed at the National Air and Space Museum in Washington, D.C.

A ticker-tape parade in New York City on June 20 was one of the events celebrating Earhart's successful transatlantic solo flight.

was in Europe, Earhart met kings and princes. On her return to the United States, she dined with President and Mrs. Herbert Hoover at the White House.

On June 21, 1932, before one of the most distinguished audiences ever assembled, President Hoover presented Earhart with the National Geographic Society's Special Gold Medal, the highest U.S. award given for geographic achievement. She was the first woman ever to receive the award. After she described her journey to those gathered, she said, "I hope that the flight has meant something to women in aviation. If it has, I shall feel it was justified." A month later in Los Angeles, Amelia received the Distinguished Flying Cross. This award, given by the U.S. Congress, honored outstanding achievement in aviation.

In the next few years, Earhart set numerous records and received many awards. Although the records and awards were not her goal, she saw them as paving the way for standard commercial air service. Her record flights kept the public aware of the growing aviation industry and showed that women belonged in aviation.

Next, Earhart planned a dangerous 2,408-mile (3,853 km) trip from Honolulu, Hawaii, across the Pacific Ocean to Oakland, California. Navigation would not be a serious problem, but the winds and weather over the Pacific were often fierce and difficult to predict.

As was her custom, A.E. planned meticulously for the flight. She looked for the best aircraft with the best engine available and bought another Vega, a Model 5C High-Speed Special, painted her favorite deep red and gold colors and powered by a Pratt and Whitney engine. This Vega carried additional fuel tanks, two-way radios, and an inflatable rubber raft.

On January 11, 1935, Amelia's heavily loaded Vega splashed down a muddy runway in Hawaii. Taking off at the last possible minute, the plane climbed over Diamond Head and headed east across the Pacific Ocean. Eighteen hours and 16 minutes later, A.E. landed in Oakland, setting

Surrounded by thousands of onlookers, Earhart climbs out of her plane following her record flight from Honolulu to Oakland.

a new record. She was the first person to fly solo from Hawaii to California. Ten thousand cheering people met her at the airport.

A.E. always made long-distance flying look easy. She would casually step into her plane, sometimes wearing a dress and a close-fitting hat instead of pants and a helmet. She set distance records from California to Mexico City and from Mexico City to New Jersey. After every flight, she urged women to share in the fun of aviation.

In June 1935, Earhart became a visiting faculty member at Purdue University in Indiana. Here she shared with students her enthusiasm for aviation and her ideas about women. She counseled female students on gaining equal status with men. She said, "We must earn true respect and equal rights from men by accepting responsibility."

Earhart's scientific approach to aviation impressed the Purdue Research Foundation. For her own research, they gave her the most advanced long-range, non-military aircraft in the world—a Lockheed Electra. In 1936, on her 38th birthday, A.E. officially took ownership of the plane. She named the shiny silver craft the *Flying Laboratory*.

The *Flying Laboratory*, Earhart's new Electra

Earhart at the controls of the *Flying Laboratory*

The all-metal Electra had two engines so if one failed, the pilot could fly with the other one. Earhart had the 10 passenger seats replaced with extra fuel tanks. This would allow the new plane to travel 4,500 miles (7,200 km) without refueling.

Now A.E. was ready for her final challenge. In 1937, she told a reporter, "I have a feeling that there is just one more good flight left in my system, and I hope this flight is it." Earhart wanted to fly around the world at the equator, a projected distance of 27,000 miles (43,200 km). Wiley Post, a famous aviator who had piloted a series of high-altitude flights, had flown around the world in 1931 and 1933, following a northern route where the land was wide and the waters were small. Post and Will Rogers, an Oklahoma humorist, were attempting a third 'round-the-world flight in 1935 when they crashed in Alaska and were both killed.

For many months, Earhart carefully planned the adventure that no one had yet attempted. Her original route was east to west. She planned to leave Oakland and fly to Honolulu and Howland Island in the central Pacific, to Port Darwin in northern Australia, and on to Africa by way of Saudi Arabia. Then she would cross the south Atlantic to Brazil and fly back to the United States.

George Putnam arranged with Standard Oil to have gasoline waiting at selected airports along her flight path and for Pratt and Whitney to supply spare engine parts at various stops. He also asked the governments of the many countries that A.E. would fly over or land at for permission use their airspace. When Amelia asked to land at Howland Island, a United States possession, her friend President Franklin D. Roosevelt issued an order to have a runway built. The order, however, was not just to help A.E. A runway on Howland Island would aid the United States in keeping an eye on the growing Japanese power in the Pacific.

Amelia hired Paul Mantz, a movie stunt flier, as her technical advisor. Maps and charts were prepared. To improve her instrument flying, Amelia spent many hours at a trainer plane that simulated various flight conditions. A special system of auxiliary tanks was designed to boost the plane's fuel capacity. Captain Harry Manning volunteered to accompany the flight as navigator. On the early sections of the flight, Commander Fred Noonan would help Captain Manning with navigation.

A.E.'s world flight began on March 17, 1937, as the *Flying Laboratory* headed west from California. Amelia flew the plane, Noonan and Manning navigated, and Mantz went along as a passenger as far as Hawaii. After a six-hour flight across the Pacific, Earhart and her team landed in Hawaii, where they rested and refueled.

The second leg of the journey was to be across the Pacific to tiny Howland Island. Because of a storm, the crew could not take off until March 20. Halfway down the runway, A.E. realized something was wrong because they were not gaining enough speed for lifting off.

Before taking off for Howland Island, Earhart's Electra had been checked over in Hawaii.

Suddenly, the plane lurched to the right. Coolly, Amelia reduced power on the left engine to halt the swing. The plane obediently nosed to the left, and, for a moment, Amelia thought she could regain control. But the Electra continued turning sharply left in an uncontrollable ground-loop. A.E. calmly cut the power switches, preventing a spark from igniting the gasoline that poured out from a ruptured wing tank. The crippled plane skidded to a stop.

No one was hurt, but the flight around the world was abruptly ended. Amelia studied the damage. The landing gear was smashed, one wing was crippled, and a wing tank was ripped open.

Amelia Earhart and Fred Noonan (top) climb out of the Electra after crashing on takeoff from Honolulu to Howland Island on March 20.

Earhart's response was the same as the one she had made when her makeshift roller coaster had dumped her on the ground many years earlier: she decided to fix the vehicle and try again.

The damaged plane was hoisted onto a boat and shipped back to California for repairs. As A.E. waited there, the best days for the flight passed. When she checked global weather patterns, Earhart found a west-to-east route would be better for a June departure. Because she still wanted to try the flight that summer, the trip had to be replanned in the opposite direction. The new route was a difficult 29,000 miles (46,400 km), or 2,000 miles (3,200 km) longer.

The crew also had to be changed. Because Captain Manning was scheduled to return to his ship, he had to drop out as navigator, and Fred Noonan had been fired by Pan American Airways because of his problem with alcohol. Nevertheless, Earhart had faith in Noonan and asked him to accompany her throughout the entire flight.

On May 20, 1937, the new flight again began at Oakland, California. This time, the repaired *Flying Laboratory* headed for Florida. But trouble was not over for Earhart and Noonan. When they landed for refueling at Tucson, Arizona, the left engine backfired and burst into flames. The damage was fixed overnight, and A.E. flew to New Orleans the next day. After a night's rest the two aviators completed the flight to Miami. During the next week, experts from Pan American made final adjustments to the plane's engines and instruments.

While the *Flying Laboratory* is made ready, A.E. and George Putnam wait in a Miami hangar, talking over plans for Earhart's second attempt to fly around the world.

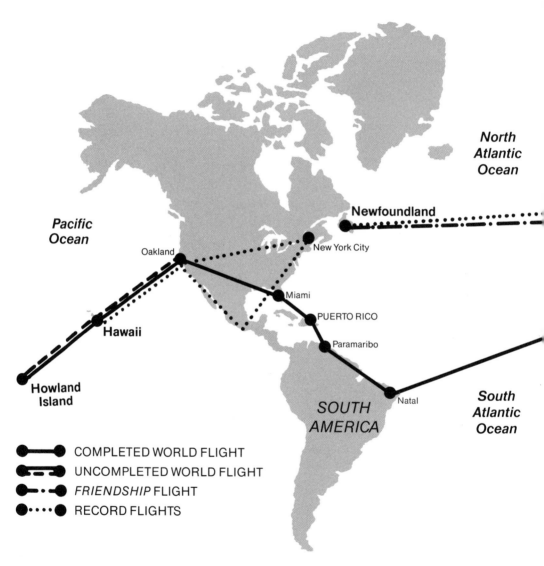

North
Atlantic
Ocean

Pacific
Ocean

Newfoundland

Oakland

New York City

Miami

Hawaii

PUERTO RICO

Paramaribo

Howland
Island

SOUTH
AMERICA

Natal

South
Atlantic
Ocean

●━━━● COMPLETED WORLD FLIGHT
●━ ━ ● UNCOMPLETED WORLD FLIGHT
●━·· ━● *FRIENDSHIP* FLIGHT
●····● RECORD FLIGHTS

Flights made by Amelia Earhart

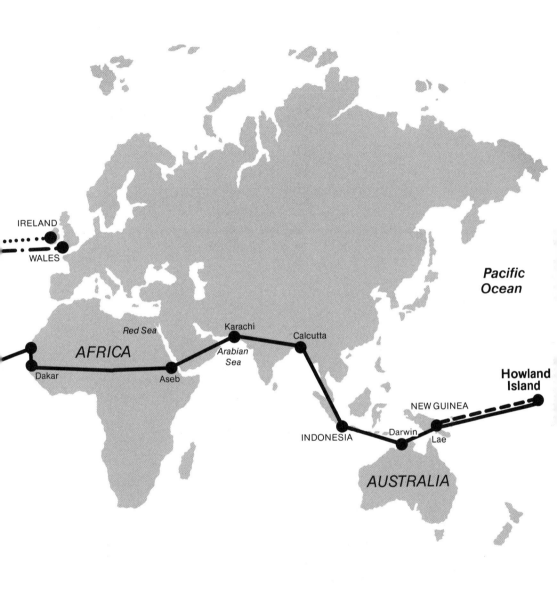

Amelia Earhart with navigator Fred Noonan in Brazil

On June 1, Earhart and Noonan left Miami. Before they reached their first stop, they heard the official announcement of the beginning of their around-the-world flight. In Puerto Rico the next morning, they learned that their second destination had to be changed. The runway at Paramaribo, Dutch Guiana, on the northeast coast of South America was being repaired. Instead, they made a shorter trip to Venezuela and waited until the runway was open again. After flying through dense rain and bucking 148-mile-an-hour winds, they finally arrived at Paramaribo. From there, a 10-hour flight over open seas and dense jungles brought the two pilots to Fortaleza, Brazil. There they had a two-day layover while mechanics overhauled the engines. On June 6, they followed the South American coast to Natal, Brazil.

The first long ocean hop loomed ahead—1,900 miles (3,040 km) across the south Atlantic to Africa. The flight went smoothly. As they approached western Africa, Noonan calculated that they needed to go south to reach Dakar, where they had planned to stop while the plane was checked again. Earhart disagreed and headed north. She was wrong. They arrived at an airport north of Dakar and had to make a brief flight to the city the next day.

On June 10, the Electra began a four-section stretch across 4,350 miles (6,960 km) of Africa. The only mishap was a buckling of the landing gear, which was fixed quickly. Then the *Flying Laboratory* headed north along the east coast of Africa to Aseb in east Africa.

The next leg was a long flight—almost 2,000 miles (3,200 km)—over Saudi Arabia and the Arabian Sea. The flight had to be nonstop because the Arabian government refused A.E. permission to land. When Earhart and Noonan did land in Karachi, India (now Pakistan), they were greeted by a British fumigation squad who feared the travelers carried yellow fever germs from east Africa. During a two-day stay in Karachi, the instruments and engines of the *Flying Laboratory* were retuned. Amelia enjoyed sight-seeing to pass the time.

On June 17, A.E. and Fred flew through heavy rains and tricky air currents to Calcutta, India. The monsoon season, which lasts from June to September, was just beginning. When they took off from the rain-drenched runway at Calcutta, the Electra's landing gear scraped against some upper branches of the trees that surrounded the airport, but no damage was done. The pair soon reached Burma, refueled quickly, and headed out into a black wall of clouds. The aviators battled monsoon rains, head winds, and no visibility for two hours before admitting they could not go on. Fred Noonan navigated the plane blindly back to Burma. The next day, the weather was no better to the east, so they backtracked to avoid the storm.

From India, Earhart and Noonan flew south through Indonesia. After a two-day delay caused by the repair of a malfunctioning long-range navigational instrument, they went on to Australia and then Lae, Papua New Guinea. Earhart now had successfully flown 22,000 miles (35,200 km).

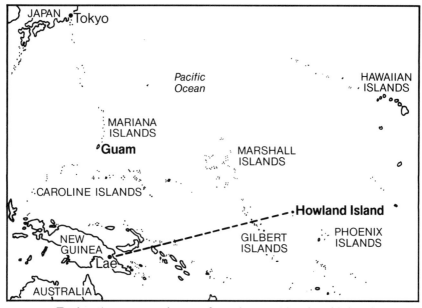

Earhart's proposed route from Lae to Howland Island

The two fliers now faced the most dangerous part of the flight. From Lae, they would head to tiny Howland Island. Only 2 miles (3.2 km) long and 1/2 mile (.8 km) wide, Howland Island juts only 20 feet (6 m) above the water. A speck in the vast ocean, the island is 2,556 miles (4,090 km) from Lae. To find Howland, precise navigation was essential. If the plane wandered north of the equator into the area of the Caroline, Mariana, and Marshall islands, it might be shot down by the Japanese. Some U.S. officials suspected a Japanese military buildup on those islands, but there was no proof because no one was permitted to fly over the Japanese-controlled waters.

U.S. fears were later proven right when the Japanese bombed Pearl Harbor on December 7, 1941, forcing the United States into World War II.

Although she never mentioned it in her accounts of the flight, Earhart's concerns over this part of the journey must have been great. To add to her worries, Noonan was having trouble with one of his navigation instruments.

At 10:30 A.M. on July 2, 1937, Amelia took off for Howland Island, relying on her luck, her instruments, and Fred Noonan. Because he had been a maritime navigator, a transport pilot, and a consultant to Pan American Airways when it mapped its routes across the Pacific, Noonan knew that part of the Pacific better than anyone else at the time. To aid the *Flying Laboratory,* three U.S. ships were stationed in the Pacific. One of them, the U.S. Coast Guard cutter *Itasca,* was sending homing signals from Howland Island. Oddly, the British authorities on the Gilbert Islands just southwest of Howland were not alerted to give her radio assistance as well.

Seven hours after takeoff, at 5:20 P.M., Amelia reported their position. They were on course and 800 miles (1,280 km) from Lae.

At 2:45 A.M. the next morning, Amelia was heard over heavy static to broadcast, "Cloudy and overcast." The radio operators on the *Itasca* sent her the weather report and the homing signal, which was the letter *A* in Morse code. At 3:45 A.M., Amelia said, "We are circling." She apparently thought they had found Howland Island. The ship's crew heard her again five hours later. She said she was flying back and forth searching for the island. The *Itasca* sent signals, but Amelia never answered. Amelia Earhart, Fred Noonan, and the Electra disappeared without a trace.

By 10:00 A.M. on July 3, the people of the world presumed that the *Flying Laboratory*'s fuel tanks would be empty, even if Amelia had conserved gasoline and encountered favorable winds. The public's hope that "Lady Lindy" would somehow find the island changed to a prayer that someone would find the fliers.

Now, the U.S. Navy began a massive sea-air search in the Pacific covering 265,000 square miles (689,000 square km). The aircraft carrier *Lexington* was sent from California to aid the *Itasca*. A long-distance navy plane, whose military duties included surveying enemy movements, flew from Hawaii to help. On its way, it ran into a bad storm north of Howland. Six more navy warships joined the hunt.

In the United States, many civilians offered their help. Ham radio operators listened and reported what they heard. The engineers at Lockheed, who had the best knowledge of the Electra's capabilities, told interviewers that Amelia's plane might survive a crash landing in the ocean. They estimated that empty fuel tanks could keep the aircraft afloat for about nine hours. George Putnam, who had been waiting in San Francisco, appealed to the Japanese consulate to ask Japanese boats to aid in the search. The Japanese did not reply.

By late July, the whole area except the parts of the Pacific controlled by the Japanese had been thoroughly searched. No clues about the disappearance of Earhart and Noonan were found. The *Lexington,* its supplies and fuel exhausted after the 15-day search, steamed back through the Golden Gate. As the ship entered San Francisco Bay, it lowered its flag to half-mast in tribute to the lost fliers.

In the next few years, many theories and rumors arose about what really happened to Amelia Earhart. One popular tale said she was captured and executed by the Japanese because she was spying on Japanese fortifications in the Pacific. This story began because Amelia was a good friend of Franklin D. Roosevelt. Plus, the U.S. military wanted to know about the activities on the Japanese islands. Also, the hostilities between Japan and the United States were increasing. Another theory suggests that Noonan was unable to navigate due to clouds and a storm. The plane then ran out of gas and crashed into the ocean.

For many years, navigators, scientists, and reporters searched the ocean and the Pacific islands for clues to Amelia's disappearance. In 1960, Fred Goerner, a CBS reporter from San Francisco, began a six-year investigation, hoping to prove that Earhart and Noonan were captured and died on Saipan, the Japanese Pacific island headquarters. In 1979, Vincent Loomis, a Florida businessman, interviewed natives of the Marshall Islands in the search for some evidence of Amelia's fate.

Anne Pellegreno, a Michigan schoolteacher, tried to find out what happened by duplicating Amelia's last flight. In 1967, Pellegreno flew a reconstructed Electra plane along the flight path planned for Earhart. She ran into dense fog near Howland, and, without modern navigational equipment, might have never found the island.

Elgen Long, a pilot and navigator from California, made a navigational flight model of Earhart's flight. He took into account many details such as the effects of crosswinds, fuel consumption data, the strength of the radio signals sent from Earhart to the *Itasca*, and the deviation of the compass on the *Flying Laboratory*. Based on this information, he is convinced that Amelia's plane ditched approximately 40 miles (64 km) northwest of Howland Island in a section of water that is about three miles deep. He hopes to use modern, deep-sea exploration equipment to recover the plane. In water that deep, the aircraft could be perfectly preserved.

Richard Gillespie, another American investigator, said he had solved the mystery of Amelia's disappearance. Gillespie works with the International Group for Historic Aircraft Recovery and has spent four years searching for information about her death. In March 1992, the search had finally uncovered two clues on the Pacific island of Nikumaroro, which is about 350 miles south of Howland Island. Gillespie found the heel of a size nine woman's shoe, thought to be of the same size and style that Amelia wore. He also found a piece of metal thought to be part

Amelia Earhart at the controls of her plane a few days before the start of her first unsuccessful 'round-the-world flight

of Earhart's plane. The National Transportation Safety Board said that this may or may not be true. Earhart and Noonan could have landed on Nikumaroro if they could not find Howland Island and were running low on fuel. Some people don't think this information is enough to solve the case, and other people do.

Whether or not the mystery of Amelia Earhart's fate is ever solved, her brilliant career is an example of what one person can accomplish. Earhart changed society's ideas about women and aviation and showed that women were capable of pioneering new fields. She proved that women could have careers in the so-called men's professions, and she aided the growing commercial aviation industry.

Throughout her life, Amelia Earhart challenged women to conquer new horizons. Before she left on her last flight, she gave a sealed letter to her husband and instructed him to open it if she did not return. In the letter she tried to explain why she undertook the dangerous 'round-the-world flight. The message was not just for her husband, for it said that women, like men, must try to do the impossible. And if they fail, their failure must be a challenge to others. Amelia Earhart was urging other women to take up where she had left off.

Amelia Earhart: Aviation Pioneer

RECORDS AND FIRSTS OF AMELIA EARHART

October 1922
Woman's altitude record of 14,000 feet (4,200 meters). Record made in a Kinner Canary, an open-cockpit, single-engine biplane.

June 17, 1928
First woman to fly across the Atlantic as a passenger. Flight made in the *Friendship,* a Fokker Trimotor monoplane with pontoons. Time: 20 hours, 40 minutes.

July 6, 1930
Woman's speed record of 181 miles per hour (290 kilometers per hour). Record made in a Lockheed Vega, a single-engine monoplane.

April 8, 1931
Autogiro altitude record of 18,451 feet (5,535 m)

May 20-21, 1932
First woman to fly solo across the Atlantic. Flight made in a 1932 Lockheed Vega, a single-engine monoplane.

May 20-21, 1932
Woman's distance record of 2,026.5 miles (3,242.4 km)

June 21, 1932
First woman to receive the National Geographic Society's Special Medal. Award given in Washington, D.C.

July 29, 1932
Only civilian to receive the Distinguished Flying Cross. Award given in Los Angeles, California.

August 24-25, 1932
Woman's nonstop transcontinental speed record from Los Angeles, California, to Newark, New Jersey. Record made in a Lockheed Vega. Time: 19 hours, 5 minutes.

July 7-8, 1933
New woman's transcontinental speed record from Los Angeles, California, to Newark, New Jersey. Record made in a Lockheed Vega. Time: 17 hours, 7 minutes.

January 11-12, 1935	First person to fly solo from Honolulu, Hawaii, to U.S. mainland, landing in Oakland, California. Flight made in Earhart's second Lockheed Vega. Time: 18 hours, 16 minutes.
April 19-29, 1935	First person to fly solo from Los Angeles, California, to Mexico City. Flight made in a Lockheed Vega. Time: 13 hours, 23 minutes.
May 8, 1935	First person to fly solo from Mexico City to Newark, New Jersey. Flight made in a Lockheed Vega. Time: 14 hours, 19 minutes.
June 1-July 3, 1937	Attempt to fly around the world at the equator. Flight made in the *Flying Laboratory*, a Lockheed Electra twin-engine monoplane. The flight was not completed.

BOOKS BY AMELIA EARHART

The Fun of It: Random Records of My Own Flying and of Women in Aviation, 1932, 1975

Last Flight, 1937 (Edited by George Palmer Putnam)

Twenty Hours, Forty Minutes: Our Flight in the Friendship, 1928, 1979

ACKNOWLEDGMENTS: The photographs are reproduced through the courtesy of: pp. 1, 5, 6, 10, Schlesinger Library, Radcliffe College; pp. 2, 22, 25, Bettmann Newsphotos; p. 7, The Kansas State Historical Society, Topeka; p. 9, Library of Congress; pp. 13, 15, Harcourt Brace Jovanovich, Inc. (from *Soaring Wings,* © 1939, 1967 by George Putnam); pp. 18, 30, 33, 34, 35, 54, Smithsonian Institution; pp. 26, 27, Seaver Center for Western History Research, Los Angeles County Museum of Natural History; pp. 28, 31, 38, 39, 41, 44, 52, AP/Wide World Photos. Front cover: Schlesinger Library, Radcliffe College. Back cover: Smithsonian Institution (left) and Don Berliner (right).